**Prepare yourself for a
jokes so wonderfully cheesy, they're
bound to make everyone smile,
groan, or maybe even both!**

With **400** jokes inside, this book is
packed with humor for every occasion.
From festive puns to unexpected
punchlines, these jokes are lighthearted,
easy to enjoy, and perfect for all ages.
Whether you're at a family gathering,
spending time with friends, or just in
need of a chuckle, this book offers a
laugh for every mood.

**Get ready to embrace the "dad joke"
spirit—where sometimes the worse
they are, the better they get!**

Holiday Jokes

Why do Christmas trees hate tests?
They always get stumped!

What does a snowman call his ex-girlfriend?
A melt-away!

How does a Christmas tree get ready for a party?
It branches out!

Why are elves so good with magic tricks?
They have elf-control!

Holiday Jokes

Why did the candy cane go to school?
To improve its "sucker skills!"

Why did the ornaments invite the lights?
They wanted to brighten the holiday!

What's a reindeer's favorite weather?
"Rain-deer!"

What did the elf say when he won the lottery?
"I'm elf-made!"

Holiday Jokes

What did the stocking say to the fireplace?
"We make the perfect pair!"

What does Santa eat on a diet?
Jelly "slims"!

What kind of photos do elves take?
"Elfies"!

Why did the Christmas tree go to therapy?
It was feeling down to its roots!

Holiday Jokes

How do elves clean
Santa's sleigh?
They give it a sleigh-vac!

What does a reindeer
put on his salad?
"Deer-essing!"

What did Santa's little helper
learn in school?
The elf-abet!

Why did Rudolph cross the road?
To say "hi" to his deer-est friends!

Holiday Jokes

What's a snowman's favorite accessory?
His cool scarf!

How does Santa's sleigh start?
With a "clause" and effect!

Why did the gingerbread man go to therapy?
He was feeling crumby!

Why did the reindeer wear bells?
Because his ant-lers needed rhythm!

Holiday Jokes

What did Santa call his lazy reindeer?
A slay-back!

How do Christmas lights
stay in shape?
By doing "circuit" training!

What did one Christmas tree
say to the other?
"Lighten up!"

Why don't snowmen get tan?
Because they're totally flake-y!

Holiday Jokes

What's a reindeer's least favorite game?
"Freeze tag!"

Why did the snowman take a break?
He needed some chill time!

Why was the Christmas tree so good at singing?
It had a great range of "pine-itches!"

How did the gingerbread man show he was brave?
He was a real tough cookie!

Holiday Jokes

What do you get when you mix a
Christmas tree and an iPad?
A pine-apple!

How do reindeer
know what day it is?
**They check the
hoof-calendar!**

Why did the elf open a bakery?
**He wanted to make
Christmas dough!**

How do snowmen
travel?
By "icicle!"

Holiday Jokes

Why did the reindeer take a nap before Christmas?
It was wiped out!

What's the Christmas tree's least favorite part of decorating?
Getting "spruced up!"

What does Santa say to the rain?
"Stop reining on my sleigh!"

Why did the Christmas candle apply for a job?
It wanted to light up someone's life!

Holiday Jokes

What does Santa put
in his lemonade?
North Poles!

Why don't snowmen get angry?
They just let it slide!

What did the reindeer say
to the carrot?
Nice to eat you!

Why did Santa put his sleigh on a diet?
It was feeling a little flakey!

Holiday Jokes

How does Santa stay so jolly?
He keeps ho-ho-hoping!

Why don't elves use smartphones?
They're all on the "Nice" list!

What goes "Oh, oh, oh"?
Santa walking backward!

What do you call Santa when he stops moving?
Santa Pause!

Holiday Jokes

Why did Rudolph bring an umbrella to Christmas Eve?
Because it was reindeer-ing!

Why was the Christmas tree so smart?
It was full of branch managers!

How do you make a Christmas tree laugh?
Tinsel it a little!

Why did the snowman stand outside?
He wanted to be cool!

Holiday Jokes

Knock, knock!
Who's there?
Stuffy.
Stuffy who?
Stuffy stocking up with treats!

Knock, knock!
Who's there?
Eve.
Eve who?
Eve-ryone's excited for Christmas!

Knock, knock!
Who's there?
Wreath.
Wreath who?
Wreath you a merry Christmas!

Knock, knock!
Who's there?
Claus.
Claus who?
"Claus" for celebration, it's Christmas!

Holiday Jokes

Knock, knock!
Who's there?
Snow.
Snow who?
Snow laughing matter, it's Christmas!

Knock, knock!
Who's there?
Holly.
Holly who?
Holly up and open the door—it's cold!

Knock, knock!
Who's there?
Wreath.
Wreath who?
Wreath you a merry Christmas!

Knock, knock!
Who's there?
Noel.
Noel who?
Noel, I don't have another gift for you!

Holiday Jokes

How does Santa's sleigh keep such good time?
It has a reindeer! (reign dear)

What did one snowflake say to the other?
"Catch you later!"

How do elves stay on top of all their tasks?
They're all very "elf-efficient!"

What's Santa's favorite workout?
Sleigh-lifting!

Nature Jokes

Why do bees hum?
Because they've forgotten the words!

Why did the spider buy a car?
To take it out for a spin.

Why did the boy wear a turtle neck sweater?
To hide his flea collar!

What is the definition of a snail?
A slug with a portable home!

Nature Jokes

What has 72 legs and catches flies?
A spider baseball team!

What do you call a greedy ant?
An anteater!

How do you hire a teddy bear?
Put him on stilts!

What do you get if you cross a skunk with a bear?
Winnie the Pooh!

Nature Jokes

Why do bears have fur coats?
Because they'd look silly in peacoats!

Why is polar bear cheap
to have as a pet?
It lives on ice!

How many bees do you
need in a bee choir?
A humdred!

What do you call a
classy ant?
Elegant!

Nature Jokes

What happened to
the cold jellyfish?
It set!

What part of a fish
weighs the most
It's scales!

Where do you find a down-
and-out cephalopod?
On squid row!

HA
HA

Why did the tree take a nap?
**It was feeling a bit
"rooted" to the spot!**

Nature Jokes

What are the
cleverest bees?
Spelling bees!

How does a bird with a broken wing
manage to land safely?
With it's sparrowchute!

What birds spend all their
time on their knees?
Birds of prey!

What do you call a
crate of ducks?
A box of quackers!

Nature Jokes

How are tigers like sergeants in the army?
They both wear stripes!

How is cat food sold?
Usually purr can!

What does a lion brush his mane with?
A catacomb!

What do chickens grow on?
Eggplants!

Nature Jokes

Who was the most famous ant scientist?
Albert Antstein!

What do you call a sick eagle?
Ill-eagle!

What do you call a very rude bird?
A mockingbird!

Why don't mountains ever get bored?
They're always "peaking" with excitement!

Nature Jokes

What do you get when a chicken lays an egg on top of a barn?
An eggroll!

Why did the turkey cross the road?
To prove he wasn't chicken!

What is the dogs favorite city?
New Yorkie!

What kind of dog chases anything red?
A bull dog!

Nature Jokes

What did one firefly say to the other?
Got to glow now!

What do you call a bee
born in May?
A Maybee!

What do you call a fly
with no wings?
A walk!

Why do plants hate math?
Because it gives them square roots!

Nature Jokes

How do you know that peanuts are fattening?
Have you ever seen a skinny elephant?

My elephant's got no trunk. How does it smell?
Terrible!

How do you take a pig to hospital?
By hambulance!

What do cows like to dance to?
Any kind of moosic you like!

Nature Jokes

What do you get if you cross a
sheepdog with a rose?
A collie-flower!

What do you get if you cross a
centipede and a parrot?
A walkie talkie!

How to fleas travel?
Itch hiking!

What did the cloud say to the sun?
"You make me evaporate!"

Nature Jokes

What do you call a pig with
no clothes on?
Streaky bacon!

What do you give
a sick pig?
Oinkment!

How do the fish get to school?
By octobus!

What fish only
shines at night?
Starfish

Nature Jokes

What do you get if you cross
a steer with a tadpole?
A bullfrog!

What is the easiest way to count a
herd of cattle?
Use a cowculator!

What kind of fly has a
frog in its throat?
A hoarse fly!

What's the ocean's
favorite type of music?
Anything with a good "wave"!

Nature Jokes

What is the strongest animal?
A snail because it carries it's home.

What do you call a rabbit with beetles all over it?
Bugs Bunny!

How did the police get rid of the bugs?
They called the S.W.A.T. team!

What did the big flower
say to the little flower?
"Hey, bud!"

Knock Knock

Knock Knock! Who's there?
March! March who?
March, march, quick, quick march!

Knock Knock! Who's there!
Philip! Philip who?
Philip the tank, I've got a long way to go!

Knock Knock! Who's there!
Anna! Anna who?
Anna one, anna two...!

Knock Knock! Who's there!
Ewan! Ewan who?
Ewan and me should get together!

Knock Knock

Knock Knock! Who's there!
Clare! Clare who?
Clare your throat before you speak!

Knock Knock! Who's there!
Heaven! Heaven who?
Heaven seen you for a long time!

Knock Knock! Who's there!
Ivory! Ivory who?
Ivory strong like Tarzan!

Knock Knock

Knock Knock! Who's there!
Diana! Diana who?
Diana thirst, can I have some water please?

Knock Knock! Who's there!
Lisa! Lisa who?
Lisa you can do is let me in!

Knock Knock! Who's there!
Disc! Disc who?
Discusting!

Knock Knock! Who's there!
Justin! Justin who?
Justin time for dinner!

Knock Knock

Knock Knock! Who's there!
Cousin! Cousin who?
**Cousin stead of opening the door
I'm still out here!**

Knock Knock! Who's there!
Dublin! Dublin who?
Dublin up with laughter!

Knock Knock! Who's there!
Ocelot! Ocelot who?
Ocelot of questions don't you!

**Knock Knock! Who's there!
Orange juice!** Orange juice who?
Orange juice going to talk to me!

Knock Knock

Knock Knock! Who's there!
Weevil! Weevil who?
Weevil only be staying a minute!

Knock Knock! Who's there!
Dinosaur! Dinosaur who?
Dino -saur with you because you called her names!

Knock Knock! Who's there!
Joan! Joan who!
Joan call us we'll call you!

Knock Knock

Knock Knock! Who's there!
Dishes! Dishes who?
Dishes your friend, so open the door!

Knock Knock! Who's there!
Nantucket! Nantucket who?
Nantucket, but she'll have to give it back!

Knock Knock! Who's there!
Actor! Actor who?
Actor you, my dear!

Knock Knock! Who's there!
Arizona! Arizona who?
Arizona room for one of us in this town!

Knock Knock

Knock Knock! Who's there!
Bean! Bean who?
Bean working very hard today!

Knock Knock! Who's there!
Eddy! Eddy who?
Eddy idea how to cure this cold!

Knock Knock! Who's there?
Modem! Modem who?
Modem lawn, the grass is getting high!

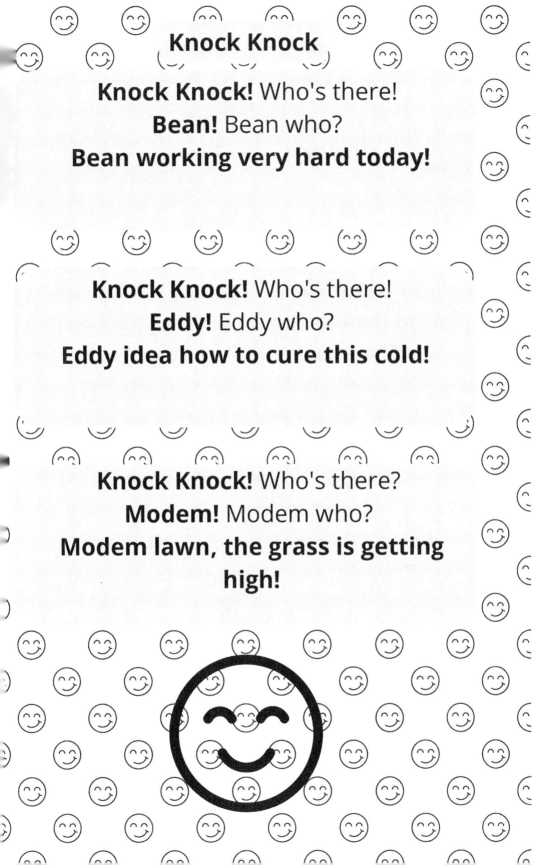

Knock Knock

Knock Knock! Who's there!
Stan! Stan who?
Stan back, I'm going to sneeze!

Knock Knock! Who's there!
Olive! Olive who?
Olive you too, honeybunch!

Knock Knock! Who's there?
Mavis! Mavis who?
Mavis be the last time I knock on this door!

Knock Knock! Who's there!
Abe! Abe who?
Abe C D E F G H...!

Knock Knock

Knock Knock! Who's there?
Matt! Matt who?
Matter of fact!

Knock Knock! Who's there!
Oliver! Oliver who?
Oliver clothes are getting wet, it's pouring out here!

Knock Knock! Who's there!
Robin! Robin who?
Robin the piggy bank again!

Knock Knock

Knock Knock! Who's there?
Curry! Curry who?
Curry me back home will you!

Knock Knock! Who's there!
Eyes! Eyes who?
Eyes got loads more knock knock jokes for you!

Knock Knock! Who's there!
Dishwasher! Dishwasher who?
Dishwasher the way I spoke before I had false teeth!

Knock Knock! Who's there!
Avocado! Avocado who?
Avocado a cold!

Knock Knock

Knock Knock! Who's there?
Manchu! Manchu who?
Manchu your food!

Knock Knock! Who's there!
Perry! Perry who?
Perry well, thank you!

Knock Knock! Who's there!
Eyesore! Eyesore who?
Eyesore do like you!

Knock, knock! Who's there?
Leaf. Leaf who?
Leaf me alone, I'm busy!

Knock Knock

Knock Knock! Who's there!
Ears! Ears who?
Ears looking at you, kid!

Knock Knock! Who's there?
Cozy! Cozy who?
Cozy who's knocking!

Knock Knock! Who's there!
Ferris! Ferris who?
Ferris fair, you win!

Knock Knock! Who's there!
Tuna! Tuna who?
**Tuna music down,
I'm trying to get some sleep!**

Knock Knock

Knock Knock! Who's there!
NE! NE who?
**NE body you like so long
as you let me in!**

Knock Knock! Who's there!
Sid! Sid who!
Sid down and have a cup of tea!

Knock Knock! Who's there!
Lettuce! Lettuce who?
Lettuce in, won't you?

Knock, knock! Who's there?
Butter. Butter who?
Butter open up, it's cold out here!

Knock Knock

Knock Knock! Who's there!
Ray! Ray who?
Ray-ning cats and dogs!

Knock Knock! Who's there!
Violins! Violins who?
Violins is the wrong way to settle an argument!

Knock Knock! Who's there!
Yoga! Yoga who?
Yoga what it takes!

Knock Knock! Who's there!
Doris! Doris who?
Doris jammed again!

Sporting Jokes

What do you get if you cross a sports reporter with a vegetable?
A common tater!

What is Dracula's favorite sport?
Bat-minton.

What sport do hairdressers love the most?
Curling!

What's a math teacher's favorite winter sport?
Figure skating!

Sporting Jokes

What is a horse's favorite sport?
Stable tennis!

What is a bugs favorite sport?
Cricket!

What sport do wasps play?
Sting-pong!

Why don't baseball players ever get lost?
Because they always follow the "base"!

Sporting Jokes

What outdoor sport do spiders like?
Fly fishing!

What's the easiest sport to get into?
Limbo, they don't set the bar very high!

What did the deer say when the sportsman asked if he wanted to go hunting?
I'm game!

I try to be a good sport, but sometimes **I'm badminton.**

Sporting Jokes

What was Viktor Frankenstein's favorite sport?
Body building!

Why don't NFL players wear glasses?
Because it's a contact sport!

What sport does the Kool-Aid man play?
Baseball, he's a pitcher!

What's a runner's least favorite animal?
A "stopwatch"!

Sporting Jokes

What's the best sport to learn when you are moving?
Boxing!

A baseball walks into Wimbledon. The announcer yells
"Hey, we don't serve you here!"

Why aren't bakeries too good at basketball?
Too many turnovers!

What do you call someone with March Madness who doesn't even like basketball?
A hypochondriac!

Sporting Jokes

Why was Cinderella thrown off the basketball team?
She ran away from the ball!

What's a basketball players favorite kind of cheese?
Swish cheese!

Why should you always take two pairs of trousers when you play golf?
In case you get a hole in one!

Why did the boxer go to the art class?
He wanted to work on his "punch" lines!

HA HA

Sporting Jokes

I paid $10 and got $20 worth of fishing supplies.
It was a net gain!

Have you seen the new fishing website?
No, it's not online yet!

What does a German soccer player call his cleats?
Das boots!

What do Greek soccer players wear?
Socra-tees!

Sporting Jokes

What did the bad soccer announcer get for Christmas?
COOOAAALLL!

What does the vampire football team eat at half-time?
Blood oranges!

What lights up a soccer pitch at night?
A soccer match!

Why did the swimmer bring extra soap to the meet?
To make a "splash"!

Sporting Jokes

Why did the football go to the bank?
To get is quarterback!

Why did the boy fail to become a
soccer player?
He didn't know how to make goals!

What dog makes a great football
player?
A golden receiver!

Why are hamburgers
essential to football?
**Because the game is played
on a griddle-iron!**

Sporting Jokes

Where do Chicago football
fans buy engagement rings?
De Beers!

What's the smartphone's
favorite football team?
The Chargers!

Why do hockey players always make
terrible birthday cakes?
Because icing is not allowed!

A limbo champion walks into a bar
and
loses their title!

Sporting Jokes

How do tennis players prefer their steak?
Wimbledon and nicely served!

You should never marry a tennis player.
Apparently love means nothing to them!

Do you remember when Ray Charles and Stevie Wonder played each other in a tennis match?
It was Endless Love!

Why did the mathematician quit his job and join NASCAR?
They told him he was good at deriving!

Sporting Jokes

What's the difference between a paddling pool and a swimming pool?
Deep ends really!

Never trust volleyball players with your drinks.
They might spike them!

What do you call refusing to go to the gym?
Resistance training!

What did the Olympian say after someone stole his sled?
What have I got to luge?

Sporting Jokes

What happened when to the
psychiatrist when they went ice
skating for the first time?
A Freudian Slip!

Why did the hipster drown?
**Because they went ice-skating
before it was cool!**

Where did the English teacher
and the student fight?
In the MLA ring!

What do race car drivers do
on their days off?
They "brake" for fun!

Sporting Jokes

Why can't Chihuahuas run marathons?
They're short of breath!

Why are soccer players never asked for dinner?
Because they're always dribbling!

Who's bad at baseball but fun at parties?
A pitcher filled with margaritas!

Why was the gymnast always so calm?
She had a lot of "balance" in her life.

Garage Jokes

Why is rust on a car orange?
Because its true car-rot!

What is an autograph?
A chart which shows car sales!

Why didn't amphibious cars ever catch on?
They were always getting toad!

Where do cars get the most flat tires?
Where there is a fork in the road!

Garage Jokes

What do you get when
dinosaurs crash their cars?
Tyrannosaurus wrecks!

What do you call a pig
behind a car wheel?
A ham brake!

What's the only painful
car rental company?
Hertz!

Knock Knock? Who's there?
Clark! Clark who?
Clark your car in the garage!

Garage Jokes

What do cars do
at the disco?
Brake dance!

What do you call a Catholic Missionary
who is also a car enthusiast?
A Catholitic Converter!

What should you do if your car's
engine is running slow?
Get it to do some Car-dio!

How do cars make new
friends?
**They just "honk" and
say hello!**

Garage Jokes

How did the motorist explain their reason for driving in their bathing suit to the police officer?
I'm in a car pool!

What did the guitarist have to drive when the electric car was getting serviced?
The acoustic!

What car does Luke Skywalker drive?
A Toyoda!

Why was the car so good at school?
It always "accelerated" in class!

Garage Jokes

What do you call a man with a car on his head?
Jack!

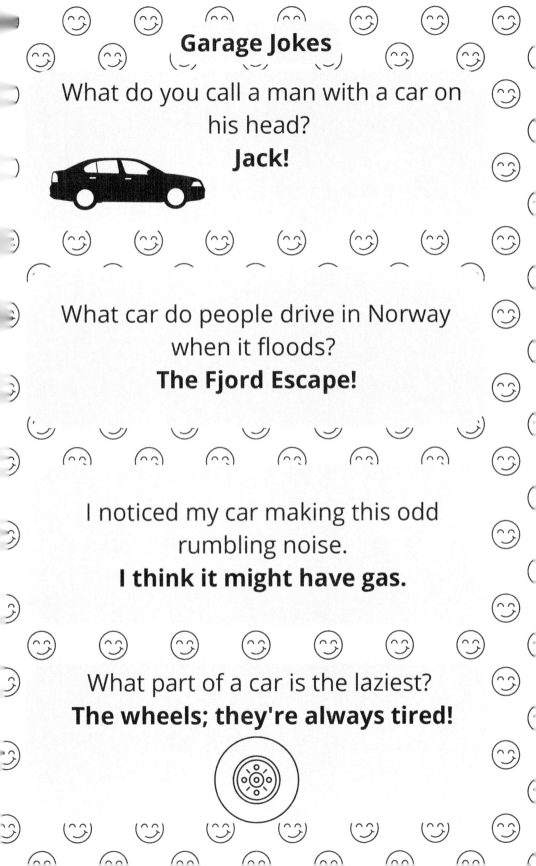

What car do people drive in Norway when it floods?
The Fjord Escape!

I noticed my car making this odd rumbling noise.
I think it might have gas.

What part of a car is the laziest?
The wheels; they're always tired!

Garage Jokes

How did the inventor of the car advertise his new "horse-less carriage"?
He said it goes without a hitch!

How do you keep a car warm in the winter?
An extra muffler!

What kind of car does a cat drive?
A Cat-illac!

What did one car muffler say to the other car muffler?
I'm exhausted!

Garage Jokes

What kind of a belly button does a German car mechanic have?
An Audi!

What kind of car does a ghost drive?
A Boogati!

What do you call a man who used to like tractors?
An extractor fan!

What did the fuel say to the car?
"I'm pumped to be with you!"

Garage Jokes

There was once a magical tractor.
It turned in to a field.

Did you hear about the new tractor movie?
I heard it has a good trailer!

I just got hired as a garbage truck driver.
There was no training, but I think I'll pick it up as I go along.

What do you do when you stub your toe?
Call a toe truck!

Garage Jokes

Why can't truck drivers
ever fully retire?
**Because they can only
semi retire!**

Why kind of motorcycles
do cows ride?
Moo-torcycles!

Why can't motorcycles
go faster?
They're two tired!

What do you get when you
mix a bush and a motorcycle?
A hedgehog!

Garage Jokes

What do you call a shop that sells aquatic vessels?
A boat-ique!

What do you call a boat made out of corn?
A tortilla ship!

Why did the young boat dock before it was ready?
Pier Pressure!

What kind of ships can't go in salt water?
Snail-boats!

Garage Jokes

Did you hear about the paddle
sale at the boat store?
It was an oar deal!

What do you call a machine that
automatically paddles your boat?
A row-bot!

Where do sick boats go?
To the dock!

What kind of car does
a bug drive?
A VW Beetle!

What train car do the ghosts always prefer to ride in?
The ca-boo-se!

What's Dracula's car called?
A mobile blood unit!

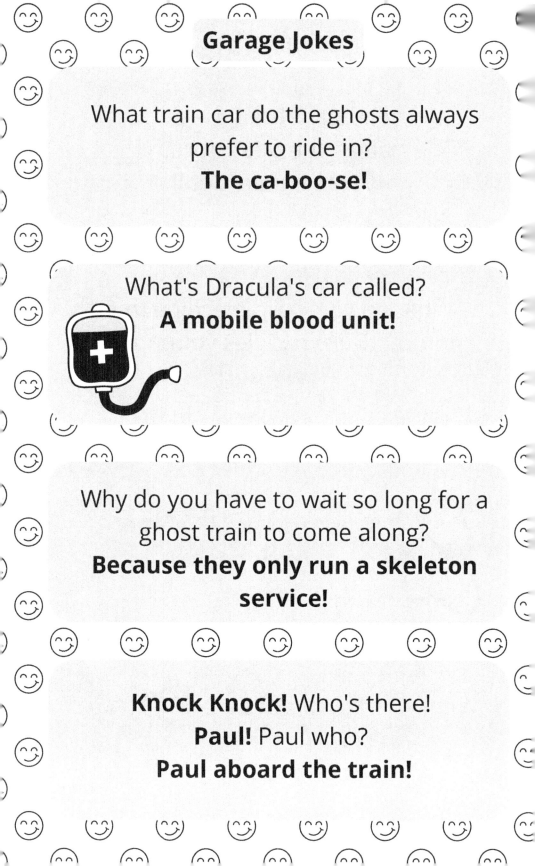

Why do you have to wait so long for a ghost train to come along?
Because they only run a skeleton service!

Knock Knock! Who's there!
Paul! Paul who?
Paul aboard the train!

Garage Jokes

Knock Knock! Who's there!
Iona! Iona who?
Iona a great train set!

What do you call a train
carrying bubblegum?
A chew-chew train!

What happens if you put
a mirror in a garage?
A mirage!

What's a mechanic's
favorite type of music?
Heavy metal!

Garage Jokes

Knock Knock! Who's there!
Tolkien! Tolkien who?
Tolkiens get you on the subway!

What is black and yellow and buzzes along at 30,000 feet?
A bee in an airplane!

What kind of cars do cats drive?
A purr-sche!

What's a car's favorite snack?
Brake-fast food!

Science & Tech Jokes

What did Mario say about Toad?
He's a fun guy!

What does a baby
computer call it's father?
Data!

What do the people of Skyrim use to
exercise?
A Nordic Track!

Why was the PC broke?
It ran out of cache!

Science and Tech Jokes

Why doesn't the elephant
use the computer?
**Because it is afraid of
the mouse!**

Why was the computer cold?
Because it left the Windows open!

What is a computer's
favorite snack?
Microchips!

What did the cell say to his
sister when she stood him up?
"Mitosis is better than this!"

Science & Tech Jokes

What do you get if you cross a
computer and a Rottweiler?
A computer with a lot of bites!

What was the spider doing
on the computer?
Searching the web!

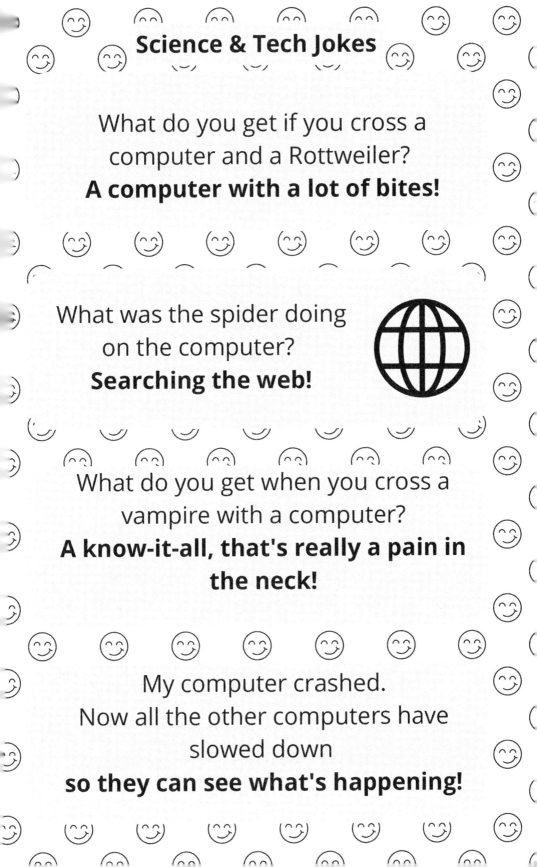

What do you get when you cross a
vampire with a computer?
**A know-it-all, that's really a pain in
the neck!**

My computer crashed.
Now all the other computers have
slowed down
so they can see what's happening!

Science & Tech Jokes

Why shouldn't you trust an atom?
Because they make up everything.

What kind of fish is made of just two atoms?
2 Na!

If our body is made of cells, what's a picture made of?
Pixels!

Why did the programmer get stuck in the shower?
The instructions said: lather, rinse, repeat!

Science & Tech Jokes

What do you get if you cross a
computer with a hamburger?
A big mac!

Why did the duck stick his leg into a
computer?
He wanted to have webbed feet!

What do couch
potatoes evolve into?
Computer chips!

Why did the computer
cross the road?
To get a byte to eat!

Science & Tech Jokes

What was eating away at the computer's RAM storage?
I don't know, but it was going at it one byte at a time!

Doctor, doctor should I surf the Internet on an empty stomach?
No you should do it on a computer!

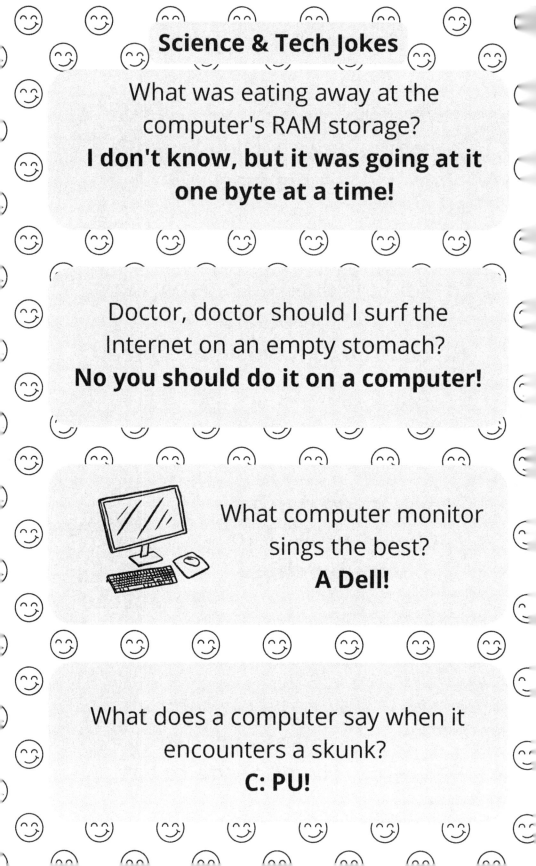

What computer monitor sings the best?
A Dell!

What does a computer say when it encounters a skunk?
C: PU!

Science and Tech Jokes

Hey, is your computer running?
Well, you better go catch it!

Why was the cookie monster arrested
for computer hacking?
**He was in possession of all the
cookies!**

Why did the computer break down?
It had a screw loose!

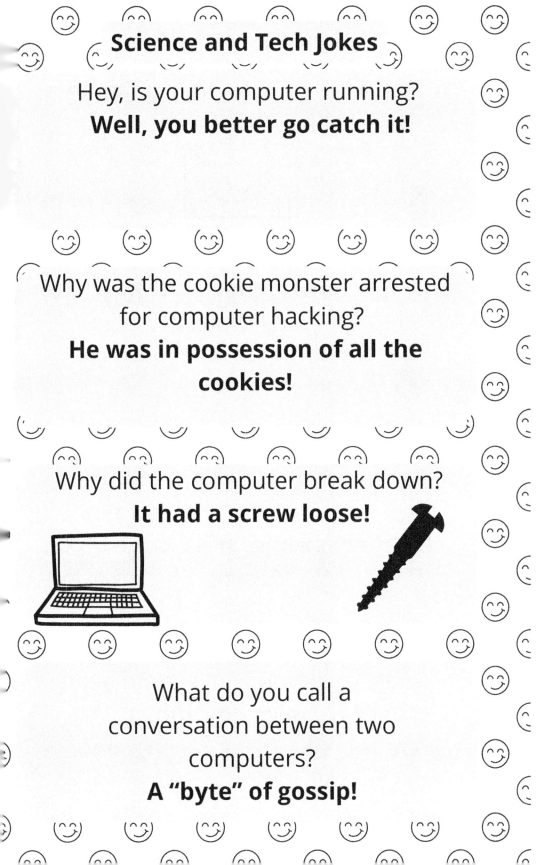

What do you call a
conversation between two
computers?
A "byte" of gossip!

What did we call IT before computers?
The Mail Room!

Why was the computer tired when he got home?
Because he had a hard drive!

I spent too much money on video games this month.
All of my savings have gone up in Steam.

What's a computer's favorite beat?
An algo-rhythm!

Science & Tech Jokes

Why did the element Fluorine in a fight?
Because it was extremely reactive!

My favorite element is Helium.
I can't speak highly enough of it!

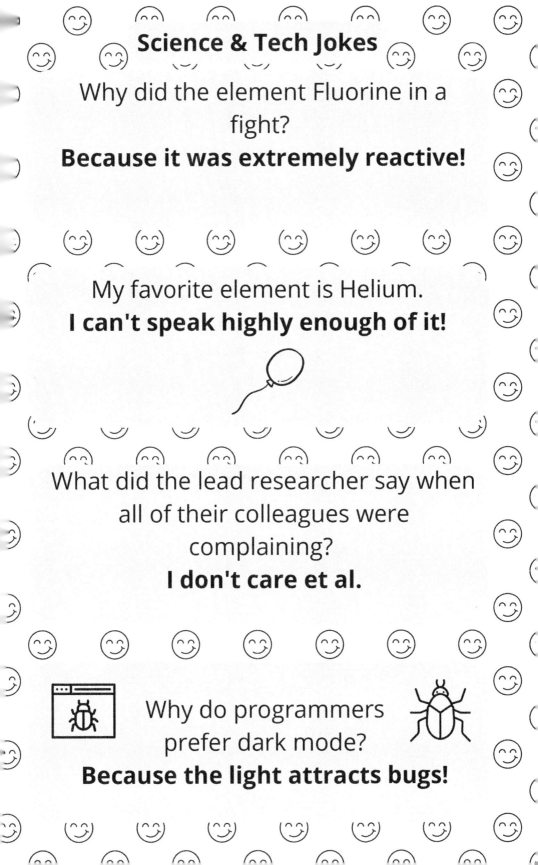

What did the lead researcher say when all of their colleagues were complaining?
I don't care et al.

Why do programmers prefer dark mode?
Because the light attracts bugs!

Science & Tech Jokes

What do you get if you stuff your computer's disk drive with herbs?
A thyme machine!

Why did the musician sell their computer?
Not enough gigs!

I received a document about the ROM in my computer science class.
It was read only.

Why did the cow go to outer space?
To visit the milky way!

Science & Tech Jokes

Knock Knock! Who's there!
Astronaut! Astronaut, who?
Astronaut here, I'll come back later!

Why couldn't the astronaut book a room on the moon?
Because it was full!

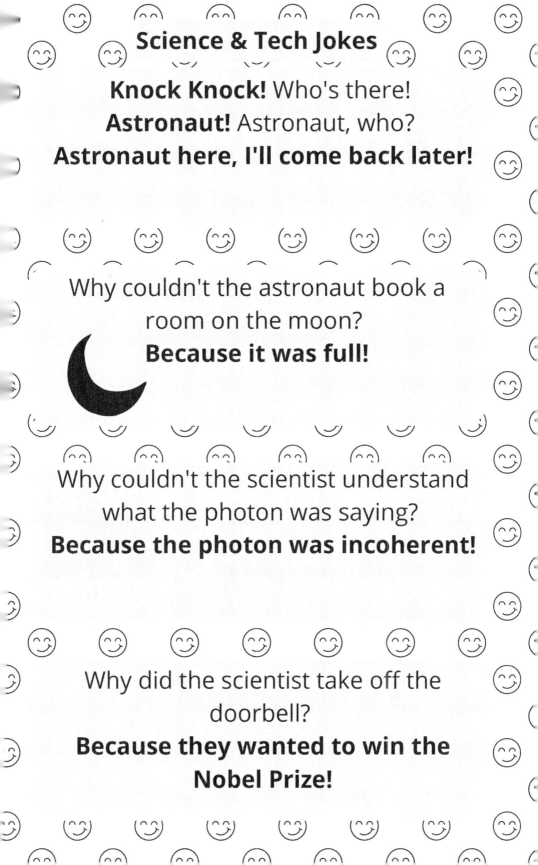

Why couldn't the scientist understand what the photon was saying?
Because the photon was incoherent!

Why did the scientist take off the doorbell?
Because they wanted to win the Nobel Prize!

Science and Tech Jokes

What's a scientist's favorite shade of blue?
Cyan-tific!

I was gonna make a chemistry joke,
but all the good ones Argon.

If you can't helium
or curium,
then you barium!

Why did the robot break up
with its software?
**It felt they weren't
"compatible" anymore.**

Science & Tech Jokes

Why do Physics and Biology teachers never get along?
Because they have no chemistry!

What do you get when you cross a sheep with a robot?
Steel wool!

Where do two electrons race?
On a circuit!

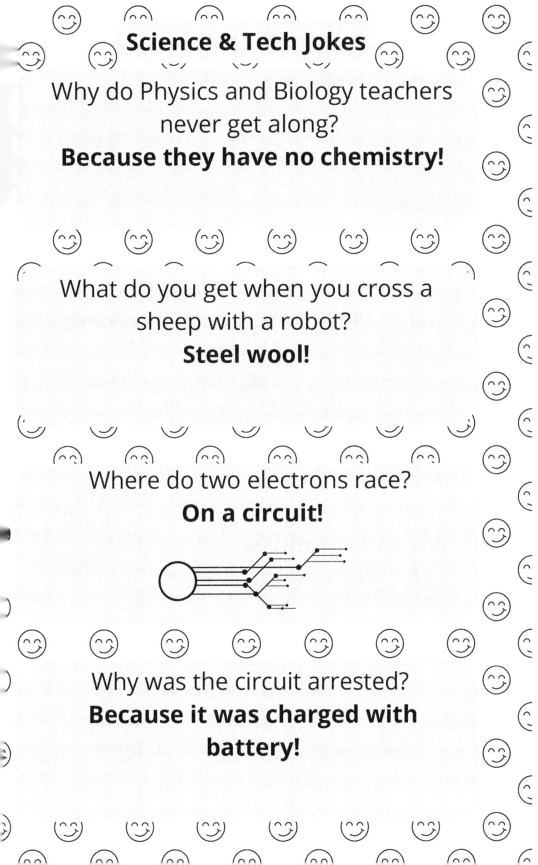

Why was the circuit arrested?
Because it was charged with battery!

What is in the red blood cells of monsters?
Hemogoblin!

I met a research geologist.
Their work was groundbreaking.

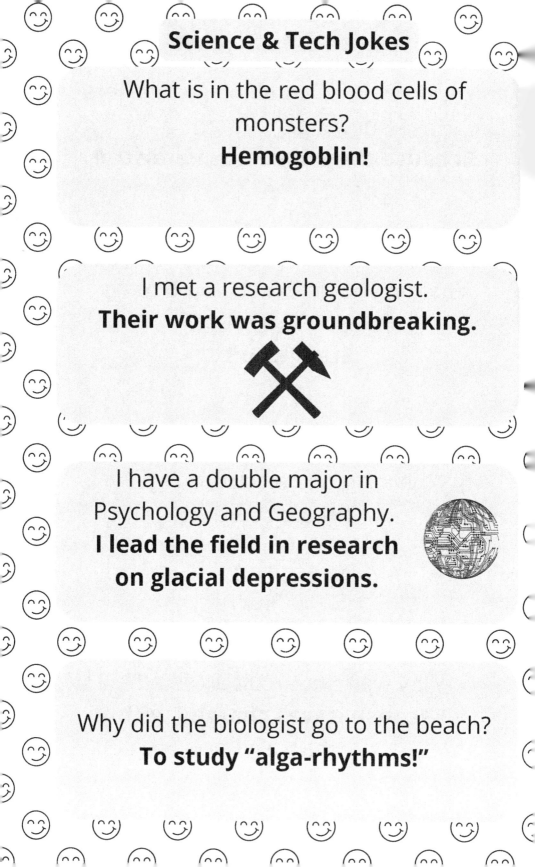

I have a double major in Psychology and Geography.
I lead the field in research on glacial depressions.

Why did the biologist go to the beach?
To study "alga-rhythms!"

Mixed Bag Jokes

What did the electrician say while swimming across a river?
Oh my, that's a lot of current!

What do you call a deep-sea diving dog?
Scuba - Doo!

How do you stop bacon from curling in the pan?
Take away their tiny brooms!

How can you can tell that a train has a gambling problem?
When it spends all its time at the track.

Mixed Bag Jokes

How does Dwayne Johnson Party?
Like a ROCK Star!

I used to work in a haunted pub.
There was spirits everywhere.

What vegetable needs a plumber?
A leek!

Why did the lightbulb get an award?
It was brilliant in every way!

Mixed Bag Jokes

What do you call two detectives tracking down a ghost?
Pair-a-normal investigators!

Did you hear about the scarecrow who won the Nobel Prize?
Apparently he was out standing in his field!

Why did the farmer make a high-pitched gasp?
Because he was tired of the sigh-low.

How do you lead a horse to water?
With carrots!

Mixed Bag Jokes

What do you call an iron cat?
A FEline.

What did the hands say to the flour?
I knead you!

They say a dog can retrieve a tennis ball from over a mile away.
Seems a bit far fetched to me.

I used to be addicted to the hokey pokey...
But then I turned myself around!

Mixed Bag Jokes

What did the fisherman say to the card magician?
Pick a cod, any cod!

What did the police do to the sweater?
They pulled it over.

If a cat won an Oscar what would he get?
An a-cat-emy award!

Why is the archaeologist sad?
Because his career is in ruins.

Mixed Bag Jokes

I burnt my Hawaiian pizza today.
I guess I should've cooked it on
Aloha temperature!

Where do most pirates come from?
Arrrrgentina!

Why do cowboys
ride horses?
**Because they're
too heavy to carry!**

Why did the painting go to jail?
Because it was framed!

Mixed Bag Jokes

What did the peanut say to the walnut?
Nothing. Nuts can't talk.

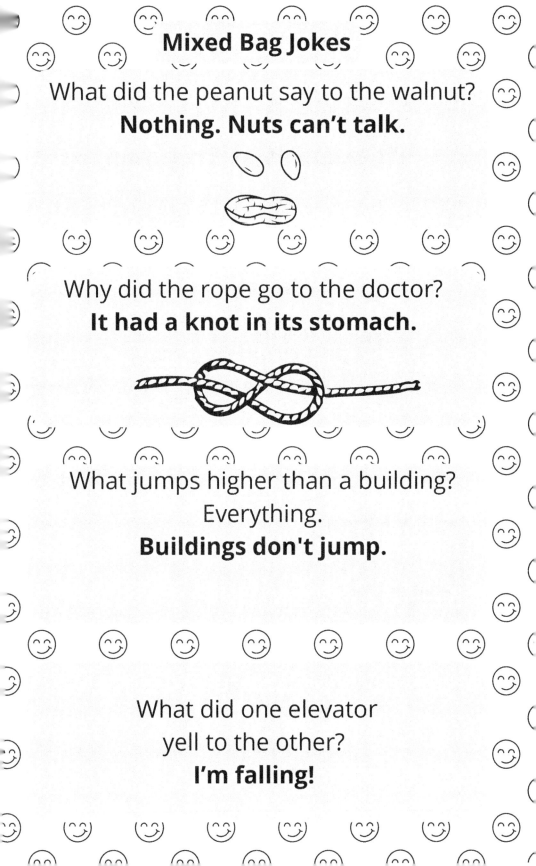

Why did the rope go to the doctor?
It had a knot in its stomach.

What jumps higher than a building?
Everything.
Buildings don't jump.

What did one elevator
yell to the other?
I'm falling!

Mixed Bag Jokes

What did one wall say to the other wall?
I'll meet you at the corner.

What did the beach say to the tide when it came in?
Long time, no sea!

What's a librarian's favorite type of bait when fishing?
Bookworms!

What do you get when you put jeans in the microwave?
Four Hot Pockets!

Mixed Bag Jokes

Where do pencils come from?
Pennsylvania!

Knock Knock! Who's there!
Bet! Bet who?
Bet you don't know who's knocking on your door!

Knock Knock! Who's there!
Pepperoni! Pepperoni who?
Pepperoni makes me sneeze!

Why did the chef break up with the cookbook?
It just didn't measure up anymore!

Mixed Bag Jokes

Did the melon get married without permission?
No, it Cantelope.

When does a joke become a dad joke?
When the joke is fully groan.

DAD

What do you call something that's impossible due to physics?
Physics-ly impossible!

Where do Polar Bears keep their money?
In the Snowbank!

Mixed Bag Jokes

What do you call a multiple choice dad joke?
A pop quiz!

What did the father lightning bolt do to his son when he misbehaved?
Grounded him!

Why are power tools good for bank robberies?
They know the drill.

Why did the man put his money in the blender?
He wanted to make some "liquid assets"!

Mixed Bag Jokes

What monsters are all the tools in the toolbox afraid of?
Vampliers!

Wanna hear my joke about pizza? **Nevermind, it's too cheesy.**

What's a minister's favorite food? **Tacos al pastor!**

Where do all the bad hamburger buns live? **In the seedy part of town!**

Mixed Bag Jokes

Which is more stable, a hamburger or a steak?
Hamburger, it's in the ground state!

My buddy is awesome at grilling steaks.
They are all very well done.

Why should you never BBQ on your roof?
The steaks are too high.

I used to be a banker, but I lost interest.
Now I'm counting on a career change!

Mixed Bag Jokes

Do you know where you get water from?
Well...

Why are trains always being falsely imprisoned?
Because of their loco motives!

What do you call a horse that lives next to you?
A Neigh-bor!

I want to give you guys my best dad joke,
but I'm afraid you won't give it back.

Mixed Bag Jokes

Why did the invisible man turn down the job offer?
He couldn't see himself doing it!

Why did the man bring string to the party?
In case he needed to "tie one on!"

I tried to catch fog yesterday...
Mist!

Why did the bread get a promotion?
It rose to the occasion!

Mixed Bag Jokes

I bought a belt that was too big...
It just went over my head!

Why did the man
sit on a clock?
**He wanted to be
on time.**

I used to be indecisive,
but now I'm not so sure.

Why did the man stare at the
can of orange juice?
Because it said "concentrate."

Printed in Great Britain
by Amazon

54588593R00059